Documents of American Democracy

ARTICLES OF CONFEDERATION

Heather Moore Niver

PowerKiDS press.

New York

Published in 2017 by The Rosen Publishing Group, Inc.
29 East 21st Street, New York, NY 10010

Editor: Katie Kawa
Book Design: Tanya Dellaccio

Photo Credits: Cover (painting) Stock Montage/Getty Images; Cover, p. 25 (document) https://commons.wikimedia.org/wiki/File:Articles_page1.jpg; Background (all pages except 25) didecs/Shutterstock.com; pp. 5, 9 (inset), 13 (right) Courtesy of the Library of Congress; p. 7 DEA PICTURE LIBRARY/Getty Images; p. 9 https://commons.wikimedia.org/wiki/File:BenFranklinDuplessis.jpg; p. 11 https://commons.wikimedia.org/wiki/File:Flickr_-_USCapitol_-_The_First_Continental_Congress,_1774.jpg; pp. 13 (left), 27 Courtesy of the National Archives; p. 15 https://commons.wikimedia.org/wiki/File:Richard_Henry_Lee_at_Nat._Portrait_Gallery_IMG_4471.JPG; pp. 17, 29 Hulton Archive/Getty Images; p. 19 https://commons.wikimedia.org/wiki/File:Articles_of_Confederation_1977_Issue-13c.jpg; p. 20 https://commons.wikimedia.org/wiki/File:US_flag_13_stars_%E2%80%93_Betsy_Ross.svg; pp. 21, 27 sjgh/Shutterstock.com; p. 23 https://commons.wikimedia.org/wiki/File:Surrender_of_Lord_Cornwallis.jpg; p. 25 (background) James Whelan/Shutterstock.com.

Library of Congress Cataloging-in-Publication Data

Names: Niver, Heather Moore, author.
Title: Articles of Confederation / Heather Moore Niver.
Description: New York : PowerKids Press, 2016. | Series: Documents of American democracy | Includes index.
Identifiers: LCCN 2016009893 | ISBN 9781499420692 (pbk.) | ISBN 9781499420715 (library bound) | ISBN 9781499420708 (6 pack)
Subjects: LCSH: United States. Articles of Confederation–Juvenile literature. | Constitutional history–United States–18th century–Juvenile literature. | United States–Politics and government–1775-1783–Juvenile literature.
Classification: LCC KF4508 .N58 2016 | DDC 343.7302–dc23
LC record available at http://lccn.loc.gov/2016009893

Manufactured in the United States of America

CPSIA Compliance Information: Batch #BS16PK: For Further Information contact Rosen Publishing, New York, New York at 1-800-237-9932

CONTENTS

A YOUNG COUNTRY BREAKS FREE

Although the United States is a young country compared to others, the U.S. Constitution is the oldest written constitution still in use anywhere in the world. However, it wasn't the first constitution written in the United States. That title belongs to the Articles of **Confederation**. In 1777, this document was adopted by the Continental Congress, but it wasn't **ratified** by all 13 states until 1781. The Articles of Confederation were used until 1789, which was when the current U.S. Constitution took effect.

Under the Articles, the United States was set up as a confederation in which each state was in charge of its own affairs. Although this document was replaced not long after it was ratified, it was an important step in the creation of the American government we know today.

The full name of the Articles of Confederation is the Articles of Confederation and Perpetual Union. "Perpetual" means "never ending."

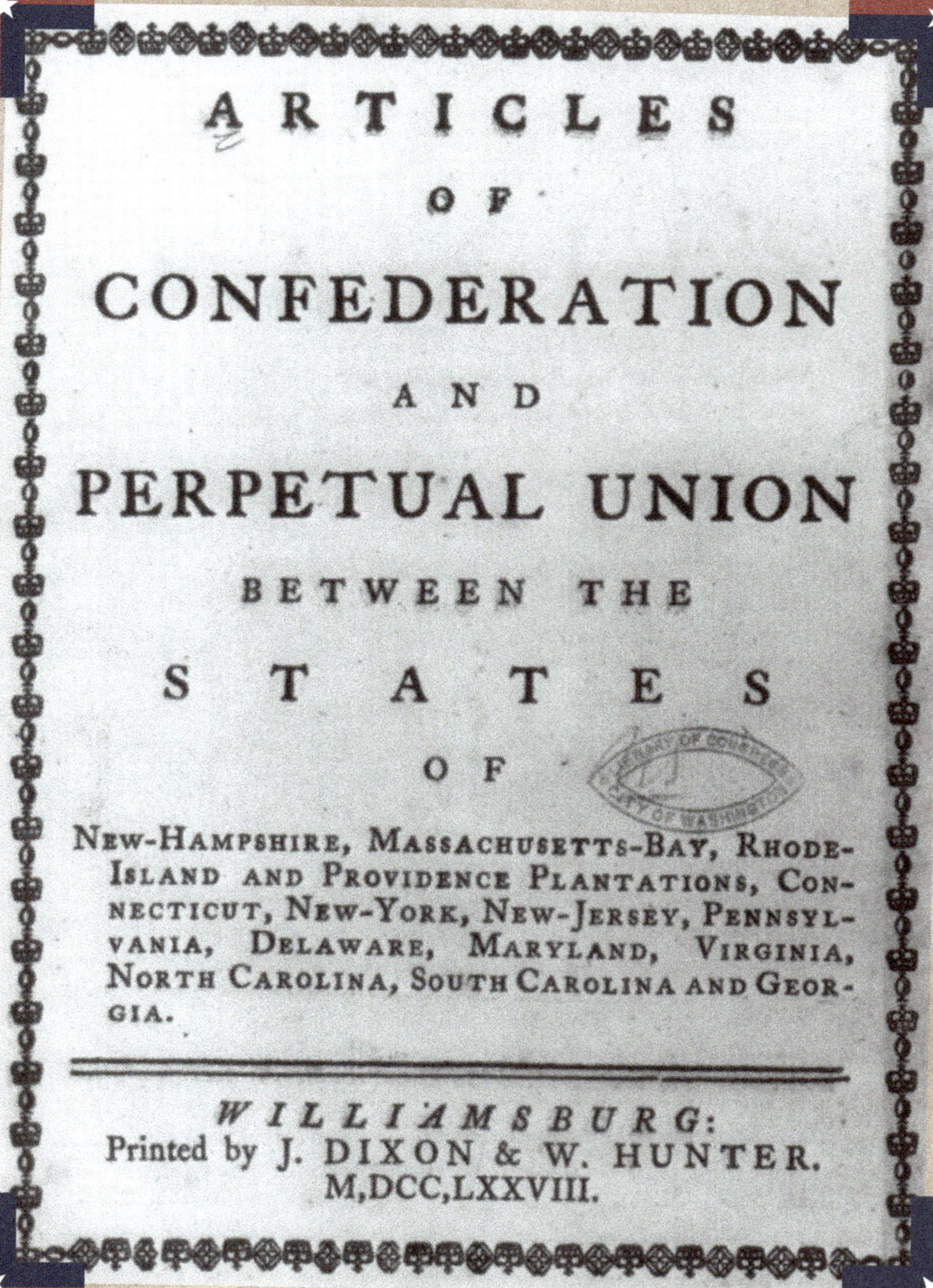

ARTICLES OF CONFEDERATION AND PERPETUAL UNION BETWEEN THE STATES OF

NEW-HAMPSHIRE, MASSACHUSETTS-BAY, RHODE-ISLAND AND PROVIDENCE PLANTATIONS, CONNECTICUT, NEW-YORK, NEW-JERSEY, PENNSYLVANIA, DELAWARE, MARYLAND, VIRGINIA, NORTH CAROLINA, SOUTH CAROLINA AND GEORGIA.

WILLIAMSBURG:
Printed by J. DIXON & W. HUNTER.
M,DCC,LXXVIII.

WARTIME WORRIES

The Articles of Confederation were written during the American Revolution. This was the war the 13 American colonies fought against Great Britain to gain their independence. Although Americans fought together toward this common goal, the American people still felt more **allegiance** to their states than to the country as a whole.

The idea of a strong central government made many Americans nervous. They didn't like the idea of their

THE AMERICAN REVOLUTION

For years, people living in the 13 colonies protested what they felt was unfair treatment by the British. They didn't like being subjected to high taxes and harsh laws without being properly represented in Parliament, or the British lawmaking body. On April 19, 1775, the divide between the colonists and the British turned violent at Lexington and Concord in Massachusetts. The American Revolution had begun. The war officially ended in 1783, when the Treaty of Paris was signed.

government having too much control over their lives. They feared this would lead to the creation of a monarchy, which is what they were trying to escape by declaring independence from the British king's rule.

U.S. leaders heard and understood these worries. With these concerns in mind, they began planning a document that would set up the government of their new nation.

The concerns that led to the American Revolution strongly influenced the creation of the Articles of Confederation.

THE ALBANY PLAN

The Articles of Confederation didn't come about after a single **draft**. A number of earlier documents inspired the Articles of Confederation. The first of these was known as the Albany Plan of Union, which was presented by Benjamin Franklin more than a decade before the start of the American Revolution. The Albany Plan—as it's often called—was meant to unite most of the colonies under one government. This group would be a loose confederation under the leadership of a president

BENJAMIN FRANKLIN

Benjamin Franklin is one of the most well-known Founding Fathers. His written contributions to the fight for American democracy include the Albany Plan and an early sketch of the Articles of Confederation. He also helped write the Declaration of Independence. During the American Revolution, Franklin worked in France, representing the United States. In addition, he helped create the U.S. Constitution we still use today. Franklin wasn't just known as a writer and public servant; he also gained fame as an inventor.

Benjamin Franklin, shown here, strongly believed the colonies needed to join together to grow stronger. The same year he proposed the Albany Plan, his newspaper, the Pennsylvania Gazette, *published this political cartoon to urge the colonies to unite.*

general and a "Grand Council." The president general would be chosen by the British king, and the council would be chosen by colonial assemblies.

The Albany Plan was adopted by the representatives to the **Albany Congress** on July 10, 1754. However, it was rejected by the colonial governments and never put into practice.

THE FIRST CONTINENTAL CONGRESS

While the Articles of Confederation set up the first formal government for the United States, a group served as a governing body before the Articles were written. In 1774, a group of male colonists formed what's now known as the First Continental Congress as a way to communicate with Great Britain and serve as the voice of the colonies. The First Continental Congress met in secret, with a total of 56 **delegates** attending from every colony except Georgia.

Joseph Galloway of Pennsylvania suggested a plan to blend British rule with some governing freedom for the colonies. This plan was turned down. Instead, the delegates decided to adopt an official statement of their rights, which also outlined the colonists' problems with British rule.

This painting, which can be seen in the U.S. Capitol, shows a meeting of the First Continental Congress.

FRANKLIN'S SKETCH

The first major step toward writing the Articles of Confederation took place on July 21, 1775. That day, Franklin submitted a sketch of his "Articles of Confederation and Perpetual Union" to the Continental Congress. Like the final accepted Articles, this document detailed 13 items, or articles, which are numbered using Roman numerals. It outlined the powers Congress should have, including the ability to set a national **currency** and decide on war and peace. Franklin also thought about the future. He included the ability to amend, or change, this document as the needs of the country changed.

Members of the Second Continental Congress talked about Franklin's document, but they never ratified it. However, it was used as a model for the Articles of Confederation that were eventually ratified and put into practice.

Shown here is part of Franklin's handwritten draft of his articles, as well as a printed version with notes by Thomas Jefferson.

NOTES AND LETTERS

We can learn a lot about the history of American democracy from studying its most important documents. In addition, there are other pieces of writing that can help us better understand those documents and what U.S. leaders thought about them. Many of the Founding Fathers took notes during meetings and wrote letters to each other. By studying these less formal pieces of writing, we can get a better sense of what early U.S. leaders thought of the young country and the documents that shaped it.

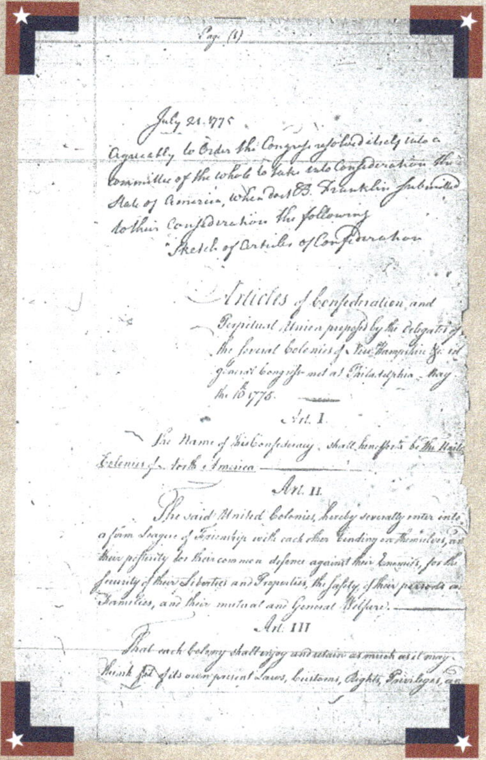

Page (1)

July 21. 1775

Agreeably to Order the Congress resolved itself into a Committee of the whole to take into Consideration the State of America, when Doct. B. Franklin submitted to their Consideration the following

Sketch of Articles of Confederation

Articles of Confederation and Perpetual Union proposed by the Delegates of the several Colonies of New Hampshire &c. in general Congress met at Philadelphia May the 10. 1775.

Art. I.

The Name of this Confederacy shall henceforth be The United Colonies of North America

Art. II.

The said United Colonies hereby severally enter into a firm League of Friendship with each other binding on themselves and their posterity for their common defence against their Enemies, for the security of their Liberties and Properties, the safety of their persons and Families, and their mutual and General Welfare.

Art. III

That each Colony shall enjoy and retain as much as it may think fit of its own present Laws, Customs, Rights, Privileges, and

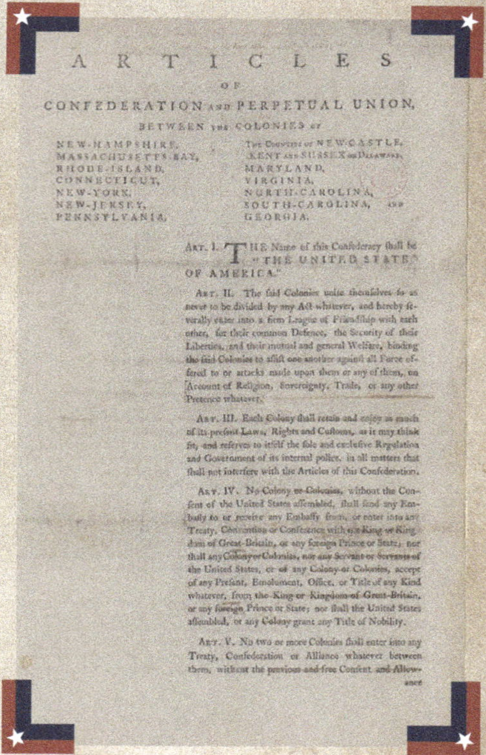

ARTICLES

OF

CONFEDERATION AND PERPETUAL UNION,

BETWEEN THE COLONIES OF

NEW-HAMPSHIRE,
MASSACHUSETTS-BAY,
RHODE-ISLAND,
CONNECTICUT,
NEW-YORK,
NEW-JERSEY,
PENNSYLVANIA,
THE COUNTIES OF NEW-CASTLE, KENT AND SUSSEX ON DELAWARE,
MARYLAND,
VIRGINIA,
NORTH-CAROLINA,
SOUTH-CAROLINA, AND
GEORGIA.

ART. I. THE Name of this Confederacy shall be "THE UNITED STATES OF AMERICA."

ART. II. The said Colonies unite themselves so as never to be divided by any Act whatever, and hereby severally enter into a firm League of Friendship with each other, for their common Defence, the Security of their Liberties, and their mutual and general Welfare, binding the said Colonies to assist one another against all Force offered to or attacks made upon them or any of them, on Account of Religion, Sovereignty, Trade, or any other Pretence whatever.

ART. III. Each Colony shall retain and enjoy as much of its present Laws, Rights and Customs, as it may think fit, and reserves to itself the sole and exclusive Regulation and Government of its internal police, in all matters that shall not interfere with the Articles of this Confederation.

ART. IV. No Colony or Colonies, without the Consent of the United States assembled, shall send any Embassy to or receive any Embassy from, or enter into any Treaty, Convention or Conference with the King or Kingdom of Great-Britain, or any foreign Prince or State; nor shall any Colony or Colonies, nor any Servant or Servants of the United States, or of any Colony or Colonies, accept of any Present, Emolument, Office, or Title of any Kind whatever, from the King or Kingdom of Great-Britain, or any foreign Prince or State; nor shall the United States assembled, or any Colony grant any Title of Nobility.

ART. V. No two or more Colonies shall enter into any Treaty, Confederation or Alliance whatever between them, without the previous and free Consent and Allowance

THE LEE RESOLUTION

It took almost a year after Franklin proposed his Articles of Confederation before any real progress was made toward drafting a formal governing plan. On June 7, 1776, Richard Henry Lee of Virginia introduced what's become known as the Lee Resolution to the Second Continental Congress.

This resolution proposed the creation of three documents. The first was a declaration of independence. The second was a plan to form alliances, or partnerships, with other countries. The final document proposed in the Lee Resolution was a "plan for confederation." Congress then created three committees to draft these documents.

The first part of the Lee Resolution was adopted by Congress on July 2, 1776. Two days later, Congress approved the Declaration of Independence. Later that year, a plan for forming alliances was passed. The Articles of Confederation were the last part of the Lee Resolution to be adopted by Congress.

Both the Declaration of Independence and the Articles of Confederation were drafted in response to the resolution introduced by Richard Henry Lee, shown here.

DICKINSON'S DRAFT

Because of the Lee Resolution, the Second Continental Congress created a committee to draft a document that could serve as a federal constitution. This committee, which was led by John Dickinson, created the first official draft of the Articles of Confederation, which was presented to the Second Continental Congress on July 12, 1776.

Dickinson's draft gave much more power to the central government than the final version of the Articles of Confederation did. In fact, his draft stated any powers not specifically given to the states belonged to the central government. This is the opposite of what's stated in both the final draft of the Articles of Confederation and the U.S. Constitution.

U.S. leaders had three major issues to debate following this draft: taxation, representation in Congress, and how the government should deal with lands to the west. These debates caused the document to change a lot from its first draft to its final form.

JOHN DICKINSON

John Dickinson served as a delegate from Pennsylvania to both Continental Congresses. He also served as a delegate from Delaware to the Constitutional Convention in 1787. Dickinson was known for his writings, including his letters and newspaper articles opposing British taxation. These were published as Letters from a Farmer in Pennsylvania, to the Inhabitants of the British Colonies. *Dickinson's talents as a writer earned him the nickname "the penman of the Revolution." He wasn't a supporter of the Declaration of Independence, but he did fight in the American Revolution.*

John Dickinson, shown here, was known as a talented writer. His writings helped shape early American democracy.

RATIFIED!

The Articles of Confederation were officially adopted by Congress on November 15, 1777. It would be several years, though, before all 13 states adopted them. Virginia was the first state to ratify the document. New Jersey, Delaware, and Maryland were the last three states to ratify it. They were worried about how it would deal with the western land claims made by larger states.

Finally, on March 1, 1781, Maryland became the last state to ratify the Articles of Confederation. This document created a confederation with a central government that didn't have much power. The states held most of the power and controlled their own affairs. The Articles also made the name of the country official: the United States of America.

Nearly five years passed between the writing of the first draft of the Articles of Confederation and its ratification by every state. This stamp shows the drafting of the Articles.

The Road Toward the Articles of Confederation

June 11, 1776	*A committee is appointed to prepare a document that unites the colonies under one government.*
July 12, 1776	*The Continental Congress receives the first draft of the Articles of Confederation.*
November 15, 1777	*The Articles of Confederation are approved by the Continental Congress.*
December 16, 1777	*Virginia becomes the first state to ratify the Articles of Confederation.*
March 1, 1781	*Maryland's delegates sign the Articles of Confederation, marking their ratification by all 13 states.*

THE FIRST FOUR ARTICLES

The 13 articles that make up the Articles of Confederation detail what was—at that time—the new government for the United States. Article I gives the United States its name. Article II declares each state is free and has its own power. If a particular power isn't specifically given to the federal government, it belongs to the states. Article III states all parts of the confederation will unite against attacks and to protect each state's freedom.

The Articles of Confederation united the 13 states under one nation. The first flag of this new country is shown here.

ARTICLE III

"The said states hereby severally enter into a firm league of friendship with each other, for their common defence, the security of their Liberties, and their mutual and general welfare, binding themselves to assist each other, against all force offered to, or attacks made upon them, or any of them, on account of religion, sovereignty, trade, or any other pretence whatever".

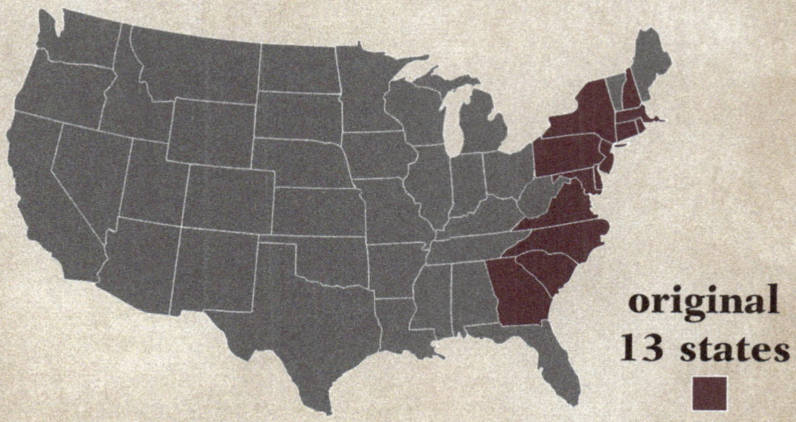

Article III of the Articles of Confederation calls for the 13 states, shown here, to enter into "a firm league of friendship with each other."

Article IV makes certain that citizens receive fair treatment in any state and can travel freely between states. The only exceptions are for "**paupers**" and "**vagabonds**," as well as criminals on the run. In the case of criminals, Article IV declares they will be returned to the state where they committed their crime.

OUTLINING POWERS

Article V of the Articles of Confederation establishes Congress itself. Each state can have from two to seven delegates, each of whom can serve for three years out of every six years. Each state's delegates must vote in a united group. This means each state has a single vote, no matter how many delegates it has.

Article VI outlines some powers the states aren't allowed to have, such as making treaties between states and building permanent armies or navies. States are required to have **militias**, but they can't declare war unless they're attacked. The officers for those militias are to be chosen by the states, according to Article VII.

Article VIII calls for a national **treasury** to be used during times of war and to help all the states. The money in this treasury comes from state taxes.

Because of the American Revolution, rules for conducting and paying for wars became important parts of the Articles of Confederation.

ARTICLE VI

"No State shall engage in any war without the consent of the united States in congress assembled, unless such State be actually invaded by enemies…."

THE FINAL FIVE

Congress's powers under the Articles of Confederation are outlined in Article IX. These include declaring war, appointing ambassadors, making treaties, and settling disagreements between states. This article also creates a Committee of States. Article X states this committee can act with the powers of Congress when Congress isn't meeting.

Article XI makes it possible for other states to join the new United States if nine states approve. Canada would have been able to join the confederation immediately.

In Article XII, the United States commits itself to paying all outstanding **debts** it had before the Articles were created. Finally, Article XIII declares the Articles of Confederation to be the law of the nation and allows for amendments if the changes are ratified by all the states.

The Articles of Confederation laid the groundwork for American democracy. Shown here are the first four articles of this document.

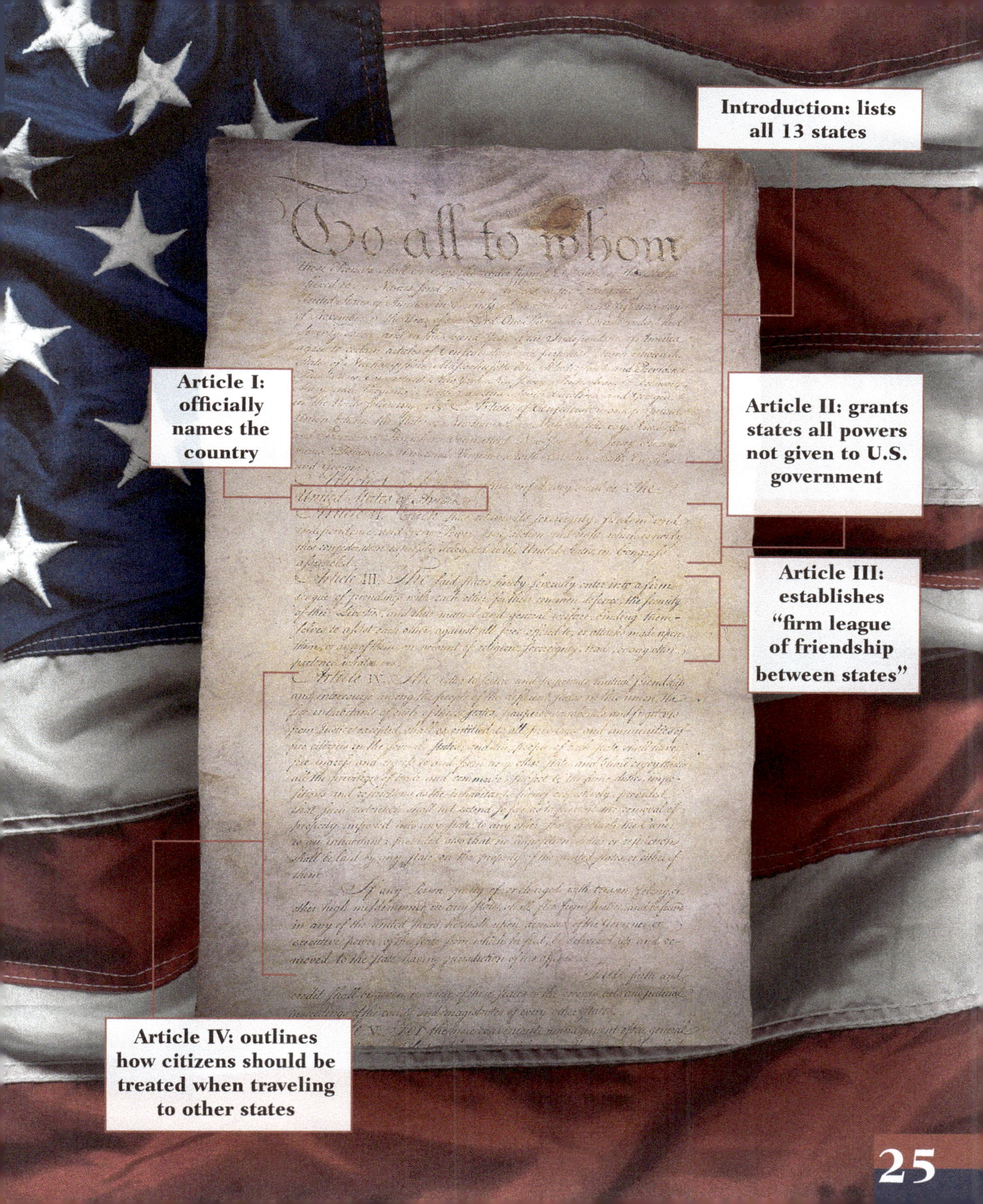

Introduction: lists all 13 states
To all to whom
Article I: officially names the country
Article II: grants states all powers not given to U.S. government
Article III: establishes "firm league of friendship between states"
Article IV: outlines how citizens should be treated when traveling to other states

STRENGTHS AND WEAKNESSES

The Articles of Confederation set up a government in which the states held most of the power. However, the central government did accomplish some important things under the Articles. Perhaps the most important was the settling of land **disputes** in the West.

In 1787, Congress passed what's commonly known as the Northwest Ordinance. This act set up the process by which lands in the Northwest Territory could become states, and it protected the rights of Americans living there.

The passing of the Northwest Ordinance was one way the central government showed its power under the Articles of Confederation. However, that power was still very limited, and its decisions couldn't be enforced. For example, Congress couldn't make the states supply money or troops to help the country as a whole.

While the central government was able to do some things under the Articles of Confederation—including passing the Northwest Ordinance, shown here—it was too weak to be truly effective.

Northwest Ordinance

An ORDINANCE for the GOVERNMENT of the TERRITORY of the UNITED STATES, North-Weſt of the RIVER OHIO.

BE IT ORDAINED by the United States in Congreſs aſſembled, That the ſaid territory, for the purpoſes of temporary government, be one diſtrict; ſubject, however, to be divided into two diſtricts, as future circumſtances may, in the opinion of Congreſs, make it expedient.

Be it ordained by the authority aforeſaid, That the eſtates both of reſident and non-reſident proprietors in the ſaid territory, dying inteſtate, ſhall deſcend to, and be diſtributed among their children, and the deſcendants of a deceaſed child in equal parts; the deſcendants of a deceaſed child or grand-child, to take the ſhare of their deceaſed parent in equal parts among them: And where there ſhall be no children or deſcendants, then in equal parts to the next of kin, in equal degree; and among collaterals, the children of a deceaſed brother or ſiſter of the inteſtate, ſhall have in equal parts among them their deceaſed parents ſhare; and there ſhall in no caſe be a diſtinction between kindred of the whole and half blood; ſaving in all caſes to the widow of the inteſtate, her third part of the real eſtate for life, and one third part of the perſonal eſtate; and this law relative to deſcents and dower, ſhall remain in full force until altered by the legiſlature of the diſtrict. ——— And until the governor and judges ſhall adopt laws as herein after mentioned, eſtates in the ſaid territory may be deviſed or bequeathed by wills in writing, ſigned and ſealed by him or her, in whom the eſtate may be, (being of full age) and atteſted by three witneſſes; —and real eſtates may be conveyed by leaſe and releaſe, or bargain and ſale, ſigned, ſealed, and delivered by the perſon being of full age, in whom the eſtate may be, and atteſted by two witneſſes, provided ſuch wills be duly proved, and ſuch conveyances be acknowledged, or the execution thereof duly proved, and be recorded within one year after proper magiſtrates, courts, and regiſters ſhall be appointed for that purpoſe; and perſonal property may be transferred by delivery, ſaving, however, to the French and Canadian inhabitants, and other ſettlers of the Kaſkaſkies, Saint Vincent's, and the neighbouring villages, who have heretofore profeſſed themſelves citizens of Virginia, their laws and cuſtoms now in force among them, relative to the deſcent and conveyance of property.

Be it ordained by the authority aforeſaid, That there ſhall be appointed from time to time, by Congreſs, a governor, whoſe commiſſion ſhall continue in force for the term of three years, unleſs ſooner revoked by Congreſs; he ſhall reſide in the diſtrict, and have a freehold eſtate therein, in one thouſand acres of land, while in the exerciſe of his office.

There ſhall be appointed from time to time, by Congreſs, a ſecretary, whoſe commiſſion ſhall continue in force for four years, unleſs ſooner revoked, he ſhall reſide in the diſtrict, and have a freehold eſtate therein, in five hundred acres of land, while in the exerciſe of his office; it ſhall be his duty to keep and preſerve the acts and laws paſſed by the legiſlature, and the public records of the diſtrict, and the proceedings of the governor in his executive department; and tranſmit authentic copies of ſuch acts and proceedings, every ſix months, to the ſecretary of Congreſs: There ſhall alſo be appointed a court to conſiſt of three judges, any two of whom to form a court, who ſhall have a common law juriſdiction, and reſide in the diſtrict, and have each therein a freehold eſtate in five hundred acres of land, while in the exerciſe of their offices; and their commiſſions ſhall continue in force during good behaviour.

The governor and judges, or a majority of them, ſhall adopt and publiſh in the diſtrict, ſuch laws of the original ſtates, criminal and civil, as may be neceſſary, and beſt ſuited to the circumſtances of the diſtrict, and report them to Congreſs, from time to time, which laws ſhall be in force in the diſtrict until the organization of the general aſſembly therein, unleſs diſapproved of by Congreſs; but afterwards the legiſlature ſhall have authority to alter them as they ſhall think fit.

The governor for the time being, ſhall be commander in chief of the militia, appoint and commiſſion all officers in the ſame, below the rank of general officers; all general officers ſhall be appointed and commiſſioned by Congreſs.

Previous to the organization of the general aſſembly, the governor ſhall appoint ſuch magiſtrates and other civil officers, in each county or townſhip, as he ſhall find neceſſary for the preſervation of the peace and good order in the ſame: After the general aſſembly ſhall be organized, the powers and duties of magiſtrates and other civil officers ſhall be regulated and defined by the ſaid aſſembly; but all magiſtrates and other civil officers, not herein otherwiſe directed, ſhall, during the continuance of this temporary government, be appointed by the governor.

For the prevention of crimes and injuries, the laws to be adopted or made ſhall have force in all parts of the diſtrict, and for the execution of proceſs, criminal and civil, the governor ſhall make proper diviſions thereof---and he ſhall proceed from time to time, as circumſtances may require, to lay out the parts of the diſtrict in which the Indian titles ſhall have been extinguiſhed, into counties and townſhips, ſubject, however, to ſuch alterations as may thereafter be made by the legiſlature.

So ſoon as there ſhall be five thouſand free male inhabitants, of full age, in the diſtrict, upon giving proof thereof to the governor, they ſhall receive authority, with time and place, to elect repreſentatives from their counties or townſhips, to repreſent them in the general aſſembly; provided that for every five hundred free male inhabitants there ſhall be one repreſentative, and ſo on progreſſively with the number of free male inhabitants, ſhall the right of repreſentation increaſe, until the number of repreſentatives ſhall amount to twenty-five, after which the number and proportion of repreſentatives ſhall be regulated by the legiſlature; provided that no perſon be eligible or qualified to act as a repreſentative, unleſs he ſhall have been a citizen of one of the United States three years and be a reſident in the diſtrict, or unleſs he ſhall have reſided in the diſtrict three years, and in either caſe ſhall likewiſe hold in his own right, in fee ſimple, two hundred acres of land within the ſame:—Provided alſo, that a freehold in fifty acres of land in the diſtrict, having been a citizen of one of the ſtates, and being reſident in the *diſtrict*; or the like freehold and two years reſidence in the diſtrict ſhall be neceſſary to qualify a man as an elector of a repreſentative.

The repreſentatives thus elected, ſhall ſerve for the term of two years, and in caſe of the death of a repreſentative, or removal from office, the governor ſhall iſſue a writ to the county or townſhip for which he was a member, to elect another in his ſtead, to ſerve for the reſidue of the term.

The general aſſembly, or legiſlature, ſhall conſiſt of the governor, legiſlative council, and
The legiſlative council ſhall conſiſt of five members, to continue in office five years, unleſs ſo
any three of whom to be a quorum, and the members of the council ſhall be nominated an
manner, to wit: As ſoon as repreſentatives ſhall be elected, the governor ſhall appoint
meet together, and, when met, they ſhall nominate ten perſons, reſidents in the diſtrict, a
in five hundred acres of land, and return their names to Congreſs; five of whom Congre
to ſerve as aforeſaid; and whenever a vacancy ſhall happen in the council, by death or
of repreſentatives ſhall nominate two perſons, qualified as aforeſaid, for each vacancy, a
greſs; one of whom Congreſs ſhall appoint and commiſſion for the reſidue of the term; an
at leaſt before the expiration of the time of ſervice of the members of council, the ſaid hou
qualified as aforeſaid, and return their names to Congreſs, five of whom Congreſs ſhall app
as members of the council five years, unleſs ſooner removed. And the governor, legiſlativ

Northwest Territory

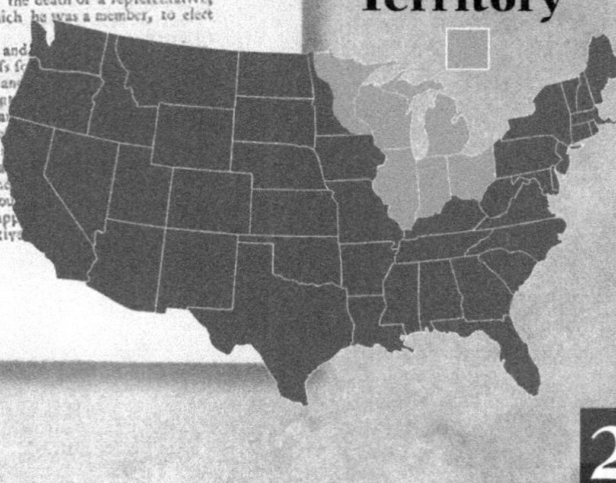

From the start, it was clear there were problems with the Articles of Confederation. It was easy for states to ignore the federal government, especially when it came to paying debts. This created an unstable financial situation in the young country.

The weakness of the central government under the Articles became even more of a problem after Shays's Rebellion, which was a violent uprising that took place in Massachusetts in 1786 and 1787. The uprising and the lack of a strong federal response to it led many to call for changes to be made to the Articles of Confederation.

In 1787, a convention was called to amend the Articles. Instead, this convention created the U.S. Constitution we use today. On March 4, 1789, this new constitution replaced the Articles of Confederation.

SHAYS'S REBELLION

Shays's Rebellion was an uprising in Massachusetts led by Daniel Shays. Shays and the men who fought with him wanted to take a stand against the taxes being raised to pay off debts from the American Revolution. Shays had served in the war, and he and other former soldiers felt these taxes were unfair. Shays led more than 1,000 men—many of them farmers—against the Massachusetts militia, but they were eventually defeated.

Shays's Rebellion opened Americans' eyes to the need for a stronger central government, which is reflected in the constitution that replaced the Articles of Confederation.

MOVING FORWARD

As the United States became its own country, its leaders had a lot to think about. They had to figure out how to best govern the new nation without giving a central government too much—or too little—power. The development of the Articles of Confederation—from the Albany Plan through many drafts based on Benjamin Franklin's first sketch—shows the country's desire to create a stable government, even while fighting a war for its freedom.

The Articles of Confederation were only officially used for eight years before they were replaced by the U.S. Constitution. However, American democracy owes a great deal to the Articles. This document allowed the new country to begin to develop a government that met the needs of its people.

GLOSSARY

Albany Congress: A meeting that took place in Albany, New York, in 1754 between representatives from seven colonies.

allegiance: Loyalty to a person, group, or cause.

confederation: A league of people or groups united for common interests or goals.

currency: Money.

debt: Money owed to another.

delegate: A person sent to a meeting or convention to represent others.

dispute: A disagreement or argument.

draft: An early version of a piece of writing. Also, to put something into written form.

militia: A group of people who are not an official part of the armed forces of a country but are trained like soldiers.

pauper: A very poor person.

ratify: To formally approve.

treasury: A place where collected funds are stored for later use.

vagabond: A person who moves from place to place without a home.

INDEX

WEBSITES

Due to the changing nature of Internet links, PowerKids Press has developed an online list of websites related to the subject of this book. This site is updated regularly. Please use this link to access the list: www.powerkidslinks.com/amdoc/arcon